I0471112

Contents

Preface

For over 15 years there have been several working capital surveys that look into the past to try and determine the future. I have been involved in a number of those published surveys and the only thing that has become an absolute truth is that the past is not a very good indicator of what will happen next. In this booklet I try to take a different angle. I will try to explain how we got to where we are and then look at the various tools, technologies and trends that are likely to affect working capital management in the coming years.

It is unlikely that all my predictions will be completely correct, but I believe that there are a number of different factors that will reshape the skills and knowledge required to manage working capital effectively.

Depending on where you are in the world and the industry in which you work only some of these factors may impact your business, but if you are unaware of the coming changes then you are more likely to become a victim of changing circumstance. Wouldn't it be better to be the early adopter that becomes the champion of the future?

Finally, I have tried to keep the language as much in laymen's terms as possible and apologise in advance where I have failed in that aim.

1 The Current State of Play

There was a time not too long ago where the average CFO or market analyst was fairly ignorant about what could be done to improve working capital results. But since then the cash flow statement has been invented and the lexicon of financial management has been embellished by terms such as Net Working Capital (NWC), Net Working Capital to Sales Ratio, Day Sales Outstanding (DSO), Days Payable Outstanding (DPO) and Days Inventory Outstanding (DIO). The implementation of ERP systems has meant that improved standardised processes have been implemented in lots of companies across the globe. The ability to record, extract and report on masses of operational transactions has transformed the capability of businesses to manage working capital.

But all these positive changes have not changed the fundamentals of the problem. With all these wonderful systems, tools and processes people are still required to use them properly. But people are fundamentally irrational. Many of the reasons for excess working capital have no basis in logic. Many supplier invoices are paid late because they never bothered to send the invoice in the first place. Customers pay late (and early) due to a lack of discipline in their own processes. Inventory is too high due to the fact that people trust their own intuition instead of the complex algorithms that have been developed to predict demand. It just doesn't make any sense.

In any one year there are roughly 30% of companies that reduce working capital and another 30% where working capital is on the increase. But year on year it is rarely the same companies making improvements or declines. It is estimated that of the world's major companies less than ten have continued to improve working capital in each of the last 15 years. So there are very few companies who really seem to understand working capital management.

For all the others the pattern can be one step forwards and then two steps backward. Circumstances can overwhelm any company. Back in late 2008 many automotive suppliers saw massive increases in inventory as revenues dropped by up to 40% in one quarter. Thankfully these events are rare, but they do happen and back then many companies were simply not ready for that scale of adjustment. The only answer for many of these firms at the time was plant closures, in many cases temporary. Most of these firms found that once demand had recovered inventories returned to their 2008 levels very quickly. This was because the plant closures drove down inventories of high selling items with stable demand patterns, but did almost nothing to affect the inventory levels of more volatile items. Once the plants opened again everything went back to the old norm. Similarly, when CFOs get their teeth into working capital receivables is often the place that they start. The perception is that receivables is more under your control than inventories and will produce results far quicker than payables. Then the memo's are sent to all the senior finance people that receivables must improve and to the amazement of the CFO these memo's seem to result in reduced receivables. But often the folks on the ground perform "heroics" in order to reach the CFO's desired targets. A favourite are year-end deals where a customer agrees to pay you very early at your year-end as long as you let things slide coming up to their year-end. In the meantime the bonuses have been paid out for improving working capital. It's only much later that senior management realise that the change in results has not been sustained. And the oldest trick in the book is stopping all supplier payments in the run-up to year-end. One factory manager once told me that he can solve his inventory problems at 3pm on the 31 December every year. Everything was shipped, but it was agreed with customers that the shipments could be returned later as part of a sale or return arrangement. But for a few key hours inventories were next to nothing.

Only a few companies have been serious about improving working capital in the long term and sustaining those improvements. They have made those improvements by streamlining processes, improving employee training, enhancing the tools available to manage working capital. They have been relentless in continually seeking further improvements beyond last year's results. But most companies have a more short term focus, so when the priorities inevitably change to other issues working capital fades into the background and old bad practices start to re-emerge. Over the years these companies often continually re-invest to solve the same problem several times.

4

2 Access to Funding

One of the major business issues of our time is small and medium sized businesses (SME's) access to funding. As banks try to repair their balance sheets they have looked to make more conservative lending decisions. As a result banks have shied away from the riskier property investments of the pre-2008 era. But for SME's things have gotten worse. In the good times their access to bank loans was already a problem and in some countries it's got to the stage where SME's almost no access to bank lending.

Instead the banks want to lend to large stable companies that already have robust balance sheets. And it's not the large companies chasing the banks for cheap loans. It's very much the other way around. While there are lots of large intelligent firms that are using the climate of cheap debt to restructure their long term debt profiles, there are many cases where banks are actively soliciting companies to borrow money they do not need. In a recent case a bank offered to factor the entire Japanese receivables book of a major FTSE 100 company at less than 1% APR. It's very difficult for large companies to turn down these lucrative offers. Even if they ultimately get a poor investment return on the money they borrowed, they only need to make sure that the return is in excess of the low borrowing cost for the transaction to justify itself. In another case, one company worked out that it was a good deal for their shareholders to borrow billions of dollars to pay for increased dividends. The shareholders were very happy with extra cash in their pockets and the share price rose dramatically. In other cases companies are giving back cash to shareholders via share buyback schemes that are again funded by debt. This suggests that these companies have run out of ideas of how to create a return for their shareholders. All of this is only possible because of the availability of cheap liquidity and the risk-averse stance of banking institutions.

The effect on working capital management has been that many large companies are not concentrating on working capital management, but are concentrating on funding. There is no doubt that if there is an opportunity to restructure long term debt super cheap rates that only a fool wouldn't do so. But there are many cases of rising levels working capital being funded by debt. There will always be cases of businesses that require more working capital in order to grow, but here we are talking about cheap debt being a substitute for better working capital management. During the dot.com bubble I remember having a conversation with the CFO of a major Dutch multinational of the time about working capital. He told me that he saw no need to improve working capital management as long as cheap debt was available. This company expanded at a phenomenal rate over a five year period and when the dot.com bubble burst they were unable to pay their debts against a profile of rapidly falling revenues. This company is now a small shadow of its former self.

Banks have transformed themselves into financial behemoths that conduct gigantic and potentially exotic financial transactions that most people in the street don't even understand. Banks have lost many of the basic skills of business banking – spotting a good business opportunity and backing it as a means to making a profit. As banks have grown bigger in the last 100 years the independence of the local bank manager has been very much reduced. Their ability to spot opportunities has faded away. This has opened up avenues for venture capitalists and private equity companies who are prepared to take controlled risks, but these guys don't have the capacity that banks have to make lending decisions that will affect the economy at large.

So in this era of cheap credit the remaining large companies that are focusing on working capital management fall into two groups. The first are those that understand that the world is changing and becoming more challenging. This might not be an immediate problem but they realise that improving working capital management in the short term will make them far more resilient companies when the expected tougher market conditions do arrive in the coming years. The other group of large companies focusing on working capital are those that are not deemed good risks by the markets and therefore have very restricted access to funds. There is always a selection of these companies at any given moment. Their need for cash is high and the pressure to improve internal processes quickly is immense. The additional stress then makes it even harder to improve and increases the chances of catastrophic failure. So planning ahead is vital for the long term health of a company.

7

3 Factoring

Invoice factoring has been going on in various forms since Mesopotamian times. Banks "buy" customer invoices at a discount from a supplier. In return the supplier gets the majority of the cash value of the invoice upfront. Factoring was a predominate form of financing in the United States textile industry right up to the early twentieth century due to the lack of large banks that could provide loans large enough to support large companies operations. These days factoring solutions are offered by banks in many countries mainly focused on smaller businesses.

In the last 10 years there has been a revolution in invoice discounting due to the establishment of web based companies that are capable of interacting with far more customers than old fashioned factoring and have the willingness to reach out to much smaller companies that the traditional factoring regimes may have overlooked. The result is that in Europe and North America it easier than ever to avail of these services. Again these services tend to be focused on smaller businesses and it has been shown that factoring can be a very expensive form of credit unless your customer base is full of blue chip customers based in countries with good credit ratings. For this reason factoring has become very much a minority activity in business although it still has its place as a very firm niche.

One of the developments of recent years is the emergence of receivables exchanges. There is one side to these businesses that is an exact replica of traditional factoring except that it is not banks who are "buying" the invoices but various types of financial institutions and even some larger companies with surplus short term cash reserves. The supplier business can potentially sell their invoices at lower discount than they would have received from the bank and the buyers can earn a modest amount on cash that otherwise would have earned them almost nothing in a traditional bank account. To succeed these exchanges depend on a constant stream of cheap liquidity coming from the buyers. When it works it can be a win-win scenario for all the players. So far this idea has made some headway in the United States and is only starting in Europe.

But the other side to these businesses is that they have spotted an opportunity to "buy" high quality invoices from major blue chip companies at a very low rate of interest. They target large quoted companies with very good debt ratings and high quality customer bases. The supplier companies are not firms that cash constrained. In fact to qualify for the lowest rates these companies need to have huge surpluses of cash. The attraction is that they can legally "sell" their current receivables, i.e. not yet due, and earn a modest rate of interest. This allows their treasury department to turn accounts receivables into a performing asset and at the same time takes a chunk of working capital off the balance sheet. The only limitation on these exchange businesses is their access to funding and market footprint of their offerings. So far these businesses have shown success in the United States but these services are emerging in Europe and other regions through the expansion of current players' footprints and the entry of new players to the market.

So if you are a large blue chip company in a country with a solid credit rating you are about to get yet another avenue to cheap and available credit. In this scenario, dependent on the jurisdiction of your company, you will also be able also be able to take these receivables off balance sheet since you are are selling them to an unrelated third party. This raises the prospect that large companies will in effect be able to deliberately understate their trade receivables positions in a perfectly legal manner.

But if you are a smaller enterprise or a larger company that is not considered to be top rated by the markets you can still participate in these exchanges but don't expect to get as cheap a funding route as your more robust large blue chip brethren. But even so these services should offer a slightly cheaper form of finance to supplier companies than traditional factoring.

So here is another opportunity that has emerged based on a mixture of technology and the availability of cheap credit that seems to be more favourable to large robust corporate than cash constrained companies.

4 Supply Chain Finance

One area of major development of the last ten years has been supply chain financing, also called reverse factoring. But as usual it is only an update on a very old idea. The history started with the issuance of different forms of bills of exchange in the eighth century AD by Chinese and Arab traders. They were designed as negotiable instruments to facilitate international trade and as such could be sold on by the bearer in order to get their cash more quickly. In the modern era the bill of exchange is no longer a major transaction type but bills of exchange and their variants are still popular in certain countries. Although not exactly the same in each country electronic bills of exchange are popular in France, confirming in Spain and promissory notes in Korea. In each case the supplier has the choice to wait to the due date and receive payment in full or obtain funds more quickly in exchange for a discount. So in that sense all these methods are forms of dynamic discounting.

Most large banks now have supply chain finance programmes that employ sophisticated software to collect supplier invoice information from the buyer and offer the seller early payment in exchange of a discount. The level of the discount should be roughly equivalent to the normal funding rate of the buyer. Therefore if you are a small company supplying a very large well funded company with a good debt rating, it should be a cheaper form of finance that you could obtain based on your own credit rating. The key to the success of these programmes is who is accepting the risk of default. For the majority of bank run programmes it will be the bank and the bank will have the power of veto over which suppliers can be part of the scheme. Unfortunately banks can be quite schizophrenic when it comes

11

to the application of these schemes. On the one hand will be the department of the bank responsible for selling the solution to buyer companies will be extremely enthusiastic about the capability of the solution and their willingness to offer the solution to the buyer. On the other hand will be the department of the bank that is responsible for lending decisions that will look at large portions of your supplier base and decide that the risk of default is beyond their very conservative algorithms and veto the supplier from the scheme. So there are many companies out there who have signed up to a supply chain finance programme, where the impact of the scheme has been very small due to these conservative risk decisions.

But now there are other structures where the buyer accepts the risk of default or where a non-bank third party accepts the risk. In these cases the schemes are much more likely to be successful since it is largely the buyer who decides which suppliers have access to the solution. For this reason even though there are dozens of banks with supply chain finance offerings, the largest player in the market currently is not a bank but a private company called Prime Revenue that has captured an estimated 10% of the global market.

But many smaller companies still continue to be sceptical about supply chain finance solutions. There is a minority that welcome the cheaper access to funding and the improved working capital position of their businesses that can result from these schemes. But there is another body of opinion that sees supply chain finance as a vehicle for larger companies to unfairly extend their payment terms. There have been a several cases where many larger companies who have already extended their payment terms in excess of 60 days and are now using supply chain finance schemes to extend their standard terms to 90 and even

120 days. Depending on which side of the fence you are on this is creating more polarised views on the subject, but it does smack of the big companies taking advantage of their position.

If these companies operate in the European Union they may encounter a problem with the latest European Union Directive on late payment (2011/7/EU). Under that directive suppliers must be paid in 60 days, with very few exceptions. And asking suppliers to accept a charge for payment in excess of 60 days may be construed as illegal. But there are two key problems with this point. Firstly, the Directive is not retrospective. So generally speaking if you as a supplier agreed to such terms before 16 March 2013 it is perfectly legal. The second problem is that the law needs to be tested in court. Similar laws have been in force in France and Spain since 2008 and there is still no case law to determine the validity of these laws or the particular circumstances where they might or might not be applied. But at face value, it looks like a problem for many supply chain management solutions.

5 Procurement Cards

Procurement cards or P-Cards have been around since the 1980's. They were originally designed for the US government as a means of eliminating costly bureaucracy. It was estimated that transaction costs could fall by up to 90% per purchase and that the vast majority of small value purchases would be suited to this kind of approach. The use of P-cards spread to the private sector in the US in the early 1990s. Private business became a big fan. Banks would send their specialist teams to the client and map all the merchant spend categories to the client's chart of accounts. This meant that all purchase orders and invoices were eliminated while a full audit record was kept that was fully acceptable for both tax and audit purposes. This success in the US market has relied on two key points – tax authorities' willingness to accept P-Card transactions as a replacement for paper invoices and the attitude to spend control that is common in the US.

On the first point, since there is no value added tax regime in the US it means that there Is no need to record and report on customer and supplier invoice transactions from an indirect taxation perspective. This has meant that the tax authorities have always been quite relaxed about accepting P-Card transactions as a replacement for paper invoices, as long as a proper audit trail is maintained.

Many US businesses have a very different attitude to control than those in other parts of the world. It is accepted that an employee could abuse the privilege of a P-Card, but the view is that any likely abuse would be so small that the net savings from the majority of users would more than cover any losses through card abuse. There are only two facts about this argument – that many businesses would agree with the point and that US newspapers regularly publish details of government officials who abuse there P-Cards on everything from weekend trips to Las Vegas to ordering too much pizza for the office party.

The European picture has been very different. There have been three broad reasons for the lack of success in Europe – tax authorities' unwillingness to accept P-Card transactions as substitute for paper invoices, businesses very different attitude to spend control and the traditionally high merchant costs.

Value added tax is applied to almost all business to business as well as business to consumer invoices across the European Union and most other European countries. As a result an invoice is a tax statement for indirect tax purposes. This has meant that tax authorities will reject a P-Card scheme unless it can produce an electronic version of each transaction as a tax invoice and that that invoice shows the line item level of detail equivalent to what is called level 3 data (e.g. goods description, units of measure, VAT coding, price per item). Most European credit card transactions are incapable of recording level 3 data. For that reason outside the United Kingdom, The Netherlands and Norway where this data can be obtained, P-Cards haven't happened at all. But even in those three countries it is up to the supplier to record the level 3 detail. If they cannot, the scheme will not be allowed. To date, there is only one solution that gets around this problem. The solution has been developed in South Africa and solves this problem comprehensively[1].

The second issue is the European attitude to spend control. The idea that employees might be allowed enough scope to behave fraudulently is an anathema to most European businesses, even if the cost of control is higher as a result. At one client, who is a large publically quoted business, all orders over €5,000 in value had be signed off by the Board of Directors and the subsequent invoice also needed to be signed off at the same level. While this is an extreme, it is an example of the preventative controls that most European businesses demand are in place.

The final point has been about merchant charges. It was not uncommon in many European countries for interchange charges to be as high as 6%! Since 2008 these charges have been falling to the point where the norm now is around 1.5% for purchase cards. There are suggestions for EU legislators that these charges should be regulated at a maximum 0.4%.

From a working capital perspective P-Cards are a win-win scenario for both the buyer and the seller. They are already successful in the USA and you should expect that success to spread further in the coming years.

6 Software

We have now spent the last 30 years upgrading ERP systems, implementing sophisticated manufacturing control technology, developing specialist pieces of software to deal with procurement, payables, receivables, inventory management and working capital reporting and so far there is only scrappy evidence that these systems really have reduced administrative costs and even less to say that they have significantly reduced working capital over the long term. That is not to say that there have not been successes, but it can be very difficult to do a post-mortem on these implementations to assess whether the expected benefits were ever realised.

The one thing that definitely is true is that all this technology has increased our businesses' capability to report on working capital movements, understand the corrective actions that may be required and monitor results to ensure that desired outcomes are fulfilled. The sad thing is that the vast majority of business users do not have the skills to make the most of these new capabilities.

A very good example would be business reporting. Most business users are reliant on standard business reports from our various systems to tell us what is going on. Many would testify that these standard reports are often not enough to understand the detail required behind some often thorny business issues. The answer was supposed to be the data warehouse. Pump lots of data from your various systems onto a giant server and then have some whizz kid write all these amazing transactional reports that would give this fine grain view of your daily business issues. In theory this does work but it is dependent on having someone with the skills to extract the right data and have a good understanding of your business so that they write reports that are relevant to the problem. This has turned out to be an uncommon mixture of skills, but without that combination businesses have spent huge sums on data warehouses without getting any real results. So people continue to spend needless hours on gigantic spreadsheets across the business world.

All this has meant that the claims of many software solutions remain true in theory but have suffered from patchy implementation. Since 2008 it is very common for finance related software packages to claim to reduce working capital. These claims have suffered from two fundamental problems.

In many cases, the software solutions are incapable of delivering a working capital benefit. A good example is purchase to pay solutions. There are many on the market that do a great job of introducing smart workflows, excellent controls and good spend reporting which should end up with a more streamlined and efficient process. But there is no evidence that these solutions are better or worse than any other solution at paying on time or reducing working capital. That's because the payment terms are controlled by the individuals who agreed the terms and many suppliers continue to be paid late because they sent their invoice to the wrong place or never sent an invoice at all. These are not issues that software can solve, so these solutions should not claim that they can.

The same can be seen with collections and dispute management software. Again there are numerous very good solutions on the market with some excellent functionality that would intuitively lead you to the conclusion that performance should improve.

However, the evidence does not bear this out. A study we ran earlier in the year[2] suggests that 5 years after implementation that 44% of clients had improved and the same number had a reduced performance. The study also showed that there was a tendency to achieve great success in the first two years after implementation; year three would see a significant drop in performance and in years four and five performance would recover, but only to half the best performance achieved in years one and two.

The bigger problem is people. As stated earlier, for these solutions to produce sustained working capital benefits people must do the right things for their organisation. But invariably people do not due to conflicting priorities derived from the fundamental dysfunctionality of many organisations with regard to working capital. Different managers are incentivised in ways that do not encourage co-operation and in some cases can encourage good people to do the wrong thing. And all this assumes that they can actually use the software solution that is provided. And if a software implementation is running over time or over budget training can be the first thing sacrificed.

7 Working Capital Reporting

In 2012 the headline was that working capital was at an all time low. In 2013 working capital has started to rise again. There are now a multitude of annual surveys that purport to tell us of some oncoming problem because the aggregate movement of working capital amongst the world's 3,000 or so largest listed companies. But these surveys are increasingly telling us the same thing from one year to the next.

The core issue about these surveys is that they have become increasingly meaningless for a number of reasons. All of these surveys concentrate on a particular region of the world or particular country. So if the survey concentrates on the top 1,000 US listed companies it can only tell me part of the truth at best. It doesn't take account of the large overseas operations of many of these companies that may be very characteristically different. For example the profile of accounts receivable in Japan, mixed up with numbers for Australia within a US parent company's numbers doesn't tell me much about trends in the US market. It only tells me about US owned assets across the world. Secondly, private companies are usually not part of these surveys since detailed data on working capital may not be available from their balance sheets. Some of the world's largest companies are in private hands, so again we do not get the full picture.

But even after putting those problems aside these surveys tend to have a huge "so what" factor about them. It is widely known by economists that working capital tends to go up in a boom as companies expand their stocks and accounts receivables in an effort to grow revenues. Equally, in a recession companies recognise the working capital risk and make great efforts to reduce stocks and accounts receivables. So in reality the results of these surveys are good indicators of whether we are in a bust or a boom, but tell us very little about whether companies in general are managing working capital better at a process level or not.

But even if you just take one company versus a range of close peers you still have a problem. Increasingly large corporations have a global footprint, but not necessarily the same footprint. For example, if you take the world's largest cement producers they are based in different countries and they are dominant in different geographical markets. It doesn't make any comparison worthless, but unless you understand the context of each producer's geographic profile the results of the comparison could be quite misleading.

A growing problem is the impact of some the latest working capital techniques on working capital. For example, if I were to compare two consumer electronics companies I might find a large difference in working capital performance. If one has implemented a successful supply chain finance programme versus the other who did not, that fact may not be obvious from published information. The same could be said for some of the other techniques mentioned earlier (factoring, P-Cards and so on). It is increasingly difficult to tell what impact these programmes have on an individual corporation. And there are international implications as well. US companies that factor their receivables in some way are obliged to disclose the fact in their quarterly reports. It can take a bit of skill to find out but it will be buried somewhere in the small print. But this is not true in many European jurisdictions where there is a need to recognise or derecognised the accounts receivable assets based on the factoring method employed, but for the outsider it is very difficult to understand whether there was a factoring transaction or not.

All this means that it is becoming increasingly difficult to use published company financial statements to make accurate comparisons of the working capital health of different companies. Does that mean we should give up on working capital comparison? I would say not since even with all the potentials for inaccuracy pointed out above the year on year trends should still be useful to financial managers. You just need to be careful about the potential expectations created by such comparisons. But that is not always a bad thing. At a major US paper company several years ago the CFO deliberately used one of these comparisons in its raw form to generate the burning platform for change that was required. It proved to be the right shock treatment and in the next 18 months they squeezed out $850 million of working capital. So these comparisons are very useful if you understand their context, but if you do not you are likely to create false expectations that will catch up you as it dawns on your colleagues that financial targets might be unachievable.

8 International Trade

One of the key issues that has been highlighted in the last year is the issue of supply chain risk. As supply chains have gotten longer in order to take advantage of manufacturing in low cost countries the number of entities in the total supply chain involved has also increased. For example, in 1990 televisions were manufactured in all of the major OECD countries. Since then the same televisions are almost all produced in China and not by the brand owners, but by contract manufacturing organisations who very often manage all or part of the supply chain independently of the brand parent. So it can be much more difficult for procurement to ascertain exactly who all the suppliers are down to the small components and services required to deliver the final product to the customer. This has exposed several major companies in the electronics and apparel industries to the risk of engaging with companies with poor safety practices, the use of child labour and the danger of invisible weaknesses in the supply chain.

We have also seen how quickly supply chain risk can impact the flow of goods. In recent years both the Japanese tsunami and the flooding in Thailand caused major disruption to the global automotive industry. Political instability is having major economic impacts in countries like Egypt and Syria but is also echoing economic impacts on neighbours such as Lebanon and Jordan. Maritime piracy seems to have declined off Somalia, but has now become a major problem off the coasts of some West African countries. But still the biggest impacts come when natural disasters hit major OECD countries. The biggest recent example would be Super Storm Sandy hitting the North-east United States. While the damage may have been fairly superficial compared to such events in other parts of the world, the economic disruption caused by power outages, fuel shortages and disruption of key shipping lanes had a much higher economic impact than almost any other event in recent times.

Another key issue in the last 30 years has been the changing pattern of trade. As mentioned earlier, a huge proportion of the rich world's manufacturing capacity has moved to low cost countries. In turn these countries have enjoyed an economic boom. As a result, wages have increased dramatically and so have property prices. In China growth started in the 1980's in the coastal special economic areas. These places have become increasingly expensive for employers to operate. The solution has been to move further into China's interior as a source of cheap labour and property. But with wage inflation in excess of 10% per year and a massive property bubble in China's industrial cities manufacturing costs are increasing at a dramatic rate. It is estimated that the cost of manufacturing in China will equal that of the United States by 2015. US companies are starting to bring back manufacturing from low cost countries (or on-shoring) to become more flexible to the needs of local demand variability. So the cost arbitrage advantage of many low cost economies is rapidly eroding.

The next issue to rear its head will be the advance of manufacturing technology. In the late 1970's robotic technology was going to usher in the next wave of efficiencies in Western economies. In 1979 Fiat brought out their famous advert for their Strada model "Hand built by Robots". The 1980's were supposed to usher in this new wave of robots that would make everything. But outside of a few select industries, such as automotive, this progression stalled as the avalanche of cheap labour available in the Far East completely changed the direction of progress in global manufacturing. But this model is starting to run out of road. That would suggest that maybe robots may be about to make a comeback and revolutionise component manufacturing. And now there is the advent of 3D printing where what are now component kits could be made in a single piece with the click from a computer. 3D printing is expected to have an increasing impact in the next five years.

This all suggests that the need to ship manufactured goods in increasingly large container ships is not going to grow at the pace that major shipping companies have predicted. Giant ships capable of carrying 19,000 containers will be available by 2017 in a market where demanding for container shipping may decline. If this becomes true then manufacturing will become more local to the consumer again. This will have huge implications for inventory management. No more weeks of stock sitting on the ocean. It should be possible to shorten lead times and reduce batch sizes so that companies can respond more flexibly to local customer demand.

9 Cash Flow Forecasting

Cash flow forecasting is always a sensitive point when talking to anyone in finance or treasury. There have been many attempts to find a solution to the problem of accurate cash flow forecasting but there always exists one fundamental problem; no one ever got fired for missing a cash flow forecast. But the pressure on organisations to become more accurate is increasing and doesn't look like going away any time soon.

But the basis of the problem has not changed that much over the years. Every business knows that there are a series of known costs that in the short term are fairly predictable; wages, salaries, taxation, debt repayments. But there are two major components of cash inflows that are very difficult to predict; accounts payable and account receivable.

It is probably more obvious that accounts receivable might be difficult to predict. Customers do not always pay on time. Often customers will pay late but early payment can be just as bad in destroying the prediction. Collectors often intuitively know which customers will pay early, late and on time but this information is rarely quantified into any predictive model.

It might be more surprising that accounts payable can be just as difficult to predict. It might seem simple for an accounts payable manager to predict what will be paid to suppliers only one week ahead. But these answers can be quite inaccurate. This can be due to delayed authorisation processes within the organisation but often it is as simple as the invoice has not yet been received from the supplier. More than 75% of all paper invoices take more than 7 calendar days between being issued by the supplier and being received by the customer. At one client we found that

26

it took 2 days longer for paper invoices to reach the shared service centre than if they had been sent to the incorrect plant address. Suppliers do this to save cost on postage or couriers and as a result can make short term payables forecasts very difficult to manage.

The one good thing that has happened in recent years is that software vendors have started to produce models that use accounts payable and accounts receivable transactional data to try and predict the exact payment and receipt dates of cash outflows and inflows. To date all these models have a basic flaw; they rely on system due dates to be accurate. The fact is, as we saw earlier, that the gap between due dates and actual payment date can be extremely erratic and these models make no attempt to try and predict the probability of on-time payment.

To address this problem, we have developed our own models to predict the actual payment dates of both payables and receivables[3]. These models borrow a thought from inventory management models that try to predict demand variability. In this case we measure the variability around the due date of the actual payment date. Thus for each payment term and each supplier it is possible to predict, within a margin of error, when payments will be early, on-time and late. The models can then be used to produce a valid forecast error measurement. Simulations show that those companies that have very stable internal processes will have lower rates of forecast error than those that have processes with less predictable outcomes. The transactions can be examined to see what is causing the forecast error, action can be taken to make the process more robust and that will lower the forecast error. Results to date have shown that highly robust processes can produce forecast errors of less than 5%. But this is a journey. Many companies suffer from short term forecast errors of up to 25%. It normally is a process of continually examining forecast error results and tweaking processes to resolve these errors before more accurate results can be derived. These models have already proved to be a huge advance on any other current available short term cash flow model.

But the Holy Grail of cash flow forecasting would be to marry up the short term forecast of the next 8 to 12 weeks, with a longer term forecast of 12 to 18 months. Our short term models do not yet answer the long term question, but with the increasing power of transactional databases and the ability to start answering the short term questions the logical progression should be that models emerge in the coming years that start to address this problem. Technology on its own is unlikely to solve these problems without input from business users and experts in forecasting techniques.

10 The Future

There have been many organisations that have been telling companies that their working capital issues are about to be solved as a direct result of their solution or service. The reality has always been that best in class working capital management is a journey that never ends. While there is clearly much more to do if you are at the start of that journey, even if you consider your organisation to be well advanced in working capital management there is always more to learn and more techniques and tools to be applied so that you stay ahead of the pack. The world is always changing be it because of competition, international trade, technology, changing market norms and legislation.

Because of the latest technologies, techniques and continuing gaps in working capital reporting requirements, it is more likely that any accurate comparison between organisations will become more difficult. This situation is unlikely to change until working capital becomes a bigger topic for those in the accounting standards community. But given that the biggest revolution in cash flow reporting – the cash flow statement – is now more than 20 years old, it is unlikely that this route of regulation is going to change at any rapid pace.

The global supply chain that has developed in the last 30 years has had major implications by lengthening the supply chain and introducing companies to new and exotic markets. The supply chain is likely to continue its evolution into something that is more locally based and more responsive to customer demand.

Equally the exotic markets of previous years have become more stable from an economic perspective. As an example, I can remember exporting goods to Cyprus and Lebanon in 1992 and we would not trade unless we could get full trade insurance against default. In the last 20 years almost all exports to these countries are on normal open terms, often without insurance. Many Asian countries used to be traded with only on letter of credit terms. This is increasing uncommon. And in other markets, such as Romania and Poland, the normal payment term norms have shortened versus the situation in the early 1990's. We expect these trends to continue.

On the payables front many large companies have done everything possible to extend credit terms and the last great movement in this direction is probably supply chain finance. Increasing regulation in the European Union and other countries makes it more likely that limits are being imposed on the maximum payment terms allowable either for particular countries or particular supplier types. In Europe, these regulations may exist but have largely not been made retrospective. So we expect that it will take several years to see these changes feed through as contracts roll over and are re-negotiated according to their natural cycle.

Cash flow forecasting will continue to be a major subject of concern, but new technologies and forecast techniques should tackle the short term forecasting problem. What will be more problematic is how the short term forecast based on transactional data and predictive techniques can be married up with the longer term forecast but progress needs to start somewhere.

30

It is a general assumption that technology is usually our friend. The great changes that have happened in working capital management in the last 30 years have been driven by the integration of systems via the ERP route and the increased ability to extract and analyse to create meaningful decision reporting. But there is still some way to go. P-Cards in Europe have in the past proved to be a false dawn, but this should change. The biggest problem is not the availability of technology for business users, but the business user's ability to use the technology to its full and create real value for their own businesses. There has been a false assumption that everyone can use technology equally, but that is as untrue as everyone's ability to shoot straight. But the key to improvement are not IT people, but technology savvy business users. This will increase the likelihood that that processes will improve, working capital will reduce and that businesses will ready for the coming wave of change.

Many of the corporate behaviours of recent years have been reacting to economic conditions rather than the general community of companies actually getting better at managing working capital. As we return to some sort of economic growth it is likely that we will see modest increases in the aggregate amount of working capital tied up on corporate balance sheets and the pattern of just as many companies increasing working capital as are reducing working capital is also likely to continue. The thing that might be a game changer is that the era of cheap debt might be nearing its end. This is unlikely to have a great effect on major corporations as they have already taken the opportunity to restructure any long term debts at very keen rates.

It will be a bigger issue for those with very highly geared balance sheets that have used cheap debt to buy cheap assets in the recession as a means of expansion. These companies will be reliant on high rates of organic growth to continue to pay down highly leveraged balance sheets.

But there will still be a continuing need to do the basics well. As economic conditions change and global economy continues to become more integrated and developed, the challenges facing working capital management will change. With more open customer payment terms, more legislation about to regulate the limits of payment terms and a shift to more localised demand management to staying ahead of the pack will remain a positive challenge.

Notes

1. The name of the P-card solution mentioned in this section is C-Solve Enterprise. This solution was developed by Integrated Commerce Solutions (ICS) in South Africa. Informita acts as an agent for ICS in Europe. More detail on the solution can be found at our website at:
http://www.informita.com/resources/Informita+-+Purchase+Cards+-+July+2013.pdf

2. Informita published a paper on the success of Accounts Receivable software in May 2013. More detail on the study can be found at our website at:
http://www.informita.com/resources/Informita+-+Collections+Software+-+May+2013.pdf

3. Informita's paper on cash flow forecasting looks at the general issues around accurate cash flow forecasting, how businesses and technology have tried to deal with the problem and how Informita's latest models deal with the problem comprehensively. Download the full review at:
http://www.informita.com/resources/Informita+-+Cash+Flow+Forecasting+-+August+2013.pdf

About the Author

Brian Shanahan is the leader and founder of Informita. Informita was formed in 2012 to assist companies in the areas of working capital and procurement, focusing on analytics, implementation and advisory. The team is there to support your working capital and procurement programmes from cradle to grave in a cost efficient and effective manner.

Before Informita, Brian spent 19 years in management consultancy, 5 years in financial accounting roles in the UK and 3 years in retail in Ireland. To date Brian has worked with over one hundred clients in 34 countries across 4 continents.

In the media, Brian has been quoted many times in the financial press in such publications as The Financial Times, CFO World, The Manufacturer, The Grocer, Finance Director, Euromoney, Accountancy Age, Financial i and The Evening Standard. Brian has also appeared on CNBC Europe's Power Lunch to discuss working capital trends.

Contacts

If you would like more information on working capital please feel to contact us in the following ways:

Website: www.informita.com

Email: info@informita.com

Phone: +44-20-3286-4109

Twitter: @informita

www.ingramcontent.com/pod-product-compliance
Lightning Source LLC
Chambersburg PA
CBHW072029190526
45166CB00015B/1669